In flight

Black Bough Poetry

Spring 2024

Guest Editor: Marcelle Newbold
Cover Artist: Emma Connolly
Editor in Chief: Matthew M. C. Smith

www.blackboughpoetry.com
Twitter: @blackboughpoems
Insta: @blackboughpoetry
FB: BlackBoughpoetry
First published by Black Bough Poetry in 2024.
Copyright ©2024

Contents

Emma Connolly is the edition's artist.

Cover art: 'In flight' front cover.

Back cover: 'Little blackbird'.
'a tiny bird… that tells a story of 21 grams, the weight of the soul'.

Guest Editor's Foreword

Hello and welcome to the Spring 2024 issue from Black Bough Poetry. It has been a pleasure to be the guest editor for 'In flight'. The poems in this issue are collated from a call-out that attracted a diverse response, with submissions through #TopTweetTuesday on Twitter, open mic slots from Black Bough online poetry nights and invited guests. It's a delight to welcome the distinguished poet Gillian Clarke to this edition. What a privilege to welcome a former National Poet of Wales.

Acute observations of the seasons, relationships, nature and moments of change are prevalent in these poems. The title and cover art came directly from the images that are explored here – movement, before and after, expectation.

'Flight':

a brilliant, imaginative, or unrestrained exercise or display
//a flight of fancy

a group of similar beings or objects flying through the air together
//a flight of geese an act or instance of running away

www.merriam-webster.com

Within the turmoil that we experience in the news, and in our day-to-day lives, we hope you enjoy these quiet moments of captured possibility.

It has been a privilege to be, once again, a small part of this gracious press and the Black Bough community.

Marcelle Newbold, guest editor, February 2024.

Veni, Vidi, Vici

A blackbird sings in the evening trees
holding his acre, his nest at its heart,
Dusk darkens the garden
as the young moon rises at its tip
a planet like a silver drop,

Nightfall, leaves stop breathing
even the blackbird's song of possession,
falls silent,
trees are sleeping.

Gillian Clarke

This Summer in the Cathedral of Bees

There is a green silence
in the cathedral of bees:
no monastic hum, no joyous treble,
no benediction of hoverfly celebrants.

The flowers wave their censers,
(garbed in new vestments,
rich with brocade)
filling the spaces between branchlet arches
with incense and invitation.

Last year I revelled in polyphony and plainchant,
marvelling at the drone and thrum
of the winged hymnal. But today
the long aisles are silent,
and the choir stalls are empty.

The wind plays toccata and fugitive song
beneath the vaulted ceiling,
as a lone chorister, small and forlorn,
hums quietly through the sacristy door
and away.

Yvonne Marjot

Echoes from Bone

His fingers atop the hollowed vulture bone
        danced over black holes, like shooting stars,
                and life-breath kissed death,

in re-creation of sun-shimmer and bird-twitter, the whistle of river,
        the sign of wind – their laughter.

Sound flowed from this relic of carrion-eater, a talisman,
        each note a step for her journey to the beyond place.

He finished and laid the flute besides her remains,
        he would wait in the cave, listen, follow the song –

bones beside bones,
echoes captured in an estuary of time.

Merril D. Smith

the gannets

the throat of the sky
has opened, she is
ruby-tongued and sliced
with the ice-white
of gannet-wing and
no-one but those
blue-eyed birds
witness me
and i – sky-drunk,
earth-bound – am nothing
more than a flicker, a wink
upon the shore

what joy, to be so
small

Rebecca Hooper

Dies irae

We go into a squall of starlings,
into sky jaundiced by thunderstorms;
hail applauding its way towards us,
the distance blurring in its white noise.

August is normally terrible
with wasps – with a heat that hangs on you
like wet wool, like a child's dressing-up.
A month of dry, taunting afternoons:

tea-stained fields, golden once with the sun
they drank in spring. Not this granite froth,
these glaucous cataracts, weighing on
exhausted air, dead as a judgement.

Mark Antony Owen

A Memory to Sustain

If a raindrop can symbolise my heart, then this
sunburnt garden, its body more weed than
grass, can contain a country. If I lay upon the
thick green, stare cloudless through a blue sky, I
will feel all I need to feel to keep my pace
constant, and head unbowed beneath a heavy
winter's night. Its memory may even sustain me
when my faith in kindness is low and the last
trace is draining down a street grid, as sirens
replace words.

David Hay

Overgrown

Elderflower offers a rack
of ivory stars,
bracken rises above thighs,
harbouring snakes and fox's eyes.

Wading through to an oak
a clearing, sheep-clipped green,
I am a tumult within
chest tight as a bite.

On a hidden path a deer
lifts its nose to scent departure.

Anna Chorlton

Hollows

We lift the hollows out of the hallowed low place
To dig deep into dry soil beside a lake
We wish to excavate to execute to resuscitate
all the parched soles   of the feet and hands
in the funereal runnels of   a ghost winter
The howling   currents   of snow I see behind
your eyes in the ice   glide   of memory
In the dark parched eyes by the soil near the lake

We take the hollows out remove the howling
from the hollow song   Come, we must move the piano
out by the cabin side under the undulating windows
To play to somersaulting clouds the north wind melodious
Trees in the path where we sit the rocks swaying conducting waves

Waves by the rocks of the rehydrating trees drinking from the hollows
The hollow, hollow spaces filling up   all lit up   with hollow songs

Robert Frede Kenter

Fishing off Swampscott Essex County MA

The seabass shoal on this
coastline like unformed thoughts
too slippery to grasp.
It is night and the moon surges with the tide;
presses closer.

She is luminous. The sand tugs
and drags, ebbs
and eddies rolling the seaweed over and over and over,
                          compressing its ink- black colour,
                                      careless of the lines we cast in hope.

We unpack the black bulk. Cast again. Mackerel
            lure the sea bass that nibble and tease then clamp their jaws
            striped and shiny
            like a new word in my mouth
            in a language I cannot pronounce.

We weigh the stripers
hold their live struggling wetness in our hands.
We measure them and return them to the ocean –
living words, we may not use.

Anne Phillips

Still Life: Contemplations on a Bust of Gandhi and a Small Twig

Look here: the fork in the road,
small as a twig in my hand.
Broken path, lingering in the silken strands
of spider art. Leaf fragment caught
on sticky thread.

Weft and warp pinion me in the crosshairs
of Summer's end.
I am a husk on the wind, sailing beyond myself
on hollow air, weightless as a seed,
fractal in search of the tree.

Gandhi frowns in bronze. His face is a forest.
I am the Handless Maiden
shedding my skin;
snake on the floor, coiled in moonlight.
My hands will grow back, bark under my nails.

Gayle J. Greenlea

The Potted Plant

Twisted, faltering, up through roots browning
into leather, the potted plant fades.
Leaves drooped, green wasted away, it sits

forlorn on a slanted wooden table,
trying to find peace with its
once forgotten brother.

Emptied of the sun and rain,
it marvels at the far off light
through dry, cracked soil and

dreams of the delicate green beyond,
seen through frosted glass
in the shadow of the hill.

Emma Jones

Sea Fever

The sea is febrile,
fretful on its grit-hard bed.

Waves tongue the shore,
cough out froth and foam.
Spittle flecks the air.

A bank of cockles
shifts and crackles.
The shells are open,
the flesh gone.

No beacon flares –
the iron lighthouse
legs rusted.

The sea withdraws
with a suffering sigh.

And all that is left
is a lone feather,
a stranded fish,
and a black dog,
running.

Iris Anne Lewis

Without borders

On our map, seas spread so far
sheets of wet air
touch great desert sands.

A hundred thousand grains
beneath bright sun
temper brisk cresting waves.

Somewhere a stray seagull
travels a pilgrim's trail,
hatches her own clutch.

Water-bird chicks
on an arid dune
peck through thin shells.

Karen Pierce Gonzalez

fissionable

how dare i speak about my aching
tree : how could i creak when we

are traipsing & you scar into the open
stares the raging street : the very

pillar of you quaking allegory of your un
intended shape a plumage shorn : a wake

of charred assumptions : form no referee
of function : your ululations yank me from

that cave of sunk beliefs : alas this ache
in you : a lake i can't undeep

Jared Mulhair

Glittering Divinity

From skyfall's strips of rust-light,
the flames of the sun's gold torch
lick ranges, edge ridges,
tongue-tip their crests,

slow.

With dusk's heaving breath,
the sky tosses its head,
divine eyelids glitter sapphire.

Matthew M.C. Smith

Haworth Triptych: Inundation

Stones slide off the moor,
tomb-tangle teeth, emerging
cliff-edged from the brackish haze
of exhumed mossy silhouttes,
eternity's throat.

Glenn Barker

Squeezing out the last drops of Summer

Bottled sunshine glows on the lunchtime table,
my Grandfather's Elderflower wine.
The faded green glass bottle,
holds the last drops of Summer.
As he pours, we all catch our breath,
knowing that the season has finished,
the final crystal sparkle shaking
on the bottle top's rim can no longer
promise happiness, youth, or wealth.
Smiles fade as we drink
to pledges we cling to,
and shiver at autumn's shadow.

Helen Openshaw

Gwal

'Rent air, lament of raptors.
Myth of Pi, radii pinned
through feather to fulcrum'.

Under this buzzard's circling shadow
the hare is frozen, mice are still,
and my trowel hand falters.
I pause, look down from heights:
she spirals up, she twists, stoops,
red hunger held. Red claws.

I wanted to preserve that moment:
I built this wall round her curves,
I drew her wings in this bend of stone,
I trowelled her flight into these rocks,
I harnessed this tunneller of clouds,
I mortared her down to my world.

When the hare runs, and mice blur,
my conceit will fall apart. Buzzards
will turn again through sky:
those captured thoughts set free.
The bird cries, she circles high:
I shake, new seer to sudden death.

Miles Hovey

And what can I wish for you?

I wish that you could
hold a little sunshine
in your palms.
Close your eyes to
summer's rush of willows
rest in seaweed dreams
under kestrel fan.
I wish you an ache
for beyond the doorstep
to fins that salt burns,
salt cleans, salt cures.
I wish you'd do what
you're afraid to do.
Live gently from one
stumble to another.

Ness Owen

Intermittent absence

Motes fluoresce in liquid air
        hang planet-like in slow waltz.

In shadow disappear, eclipsed
        by dusk's sleight-of-hand

until low sun tilts shade,
        flames pin-point stars to life.

There-and-not-there, these sly celestial specks
        whose tricks you learned.

Lesley Curwen

Though hawthorns walk beside me

Inside the tangled forest
a breath of indigo wind
shadows gather leaves from a roughshod earth

in the paisley hours of orchid willow
tree hollows make room for nightfall
and the evening's hourglass drains its last star

something in the sage air leaps

and the wind curls figure-eights

into silk scarves

Regine Ebner

Attracted to light

Oh how stillness is valued.
Steady ship, solid base.

As if a wobble, a lack of consistent
dampening down of fluctuations

is undesirable. Yesterday
I witnessed a beautiful tree.

Three moths winged into my back
dominoed by abrupt lack

of movement. Still, I gawped.
I house them here now

they occupy
urge me off balance.

Marcelle Newbold

August

Pink shouldered, red nosed August
hands over ninety-nines and fresh dried donuts,
slips you a fiver when your mum's not looking,
smells of vanilla, cigarettes, and cider.

Patient August, sitting in the car,
winding the windows down, she's sweating,
cracking jokes and singing,
hot thighs sticking to the plastic seat.

Generous August, gathering blackberries
in a spare plastic bag, and eating them
forgetfully, with fingers purple-tipped –
laughing August, kiss-me-quick and squeeze-me-slow,
finding the windbreak, cutting sandwiches –
cheese or ham? – throwing in crisps and pop –

and under that creased skirt,
the scratch of stubbled fields,
a young fox creeping through the hedge, a hare
running and leaping wild beneath
a golden moon.

Sarah Connor

Roadside

Leaving the tarmac, straying onto the verge
wearing crisp wellies, our fingertips reach
curve round the untidy grass cup

a mottled brown-blue egg, jagged edge
eggshell, where a blackbird tucked in tight
once breathed through inside

released from the white membrane
unseen fledgling notes in the wild garlic

Jo Dixon

Chai

She no longer thinks about it. Hot water
and milk, 2:1. Steel pot, lighter, stove-top,
flame.

Then the blood-saffron, just a strand.
Seeds of fennel in wrinkled hand, cardamom
crushed, fragrant. A bay leaf that smells
of home. Not this one.

Yellow fingers sift tea leaves,
fine and shrivelled
like dried up dreams.

The sugar pot's lid is chipped.
Like her husband's spirit: sliced
by a line on the map.

Truth is a homeland stolen by ink
a border you will not cross twice.
A woman is born to endure, her mother said-
little did she know.

Steam swirls: Lahore's rose-pink dawn,
ghosts of sisters killed and lost.
She pours and sieves
a blood potion for those who survive.

'Chai!' he booms from the living room
she adds sugar and stirs-
remembers her sisters and lets them go.

Saraswati Nagpal

Recommended reading

Check out these titles from the Bough and friends:

The Black Bough Poetry Library
(all titles available on Amazon)

2020

Deep Time Vol 1 anthology
Deep Time Vol 2 anthology
Christmas & Winter Vol 1 anthology

2021

Christmas & Winter Vol 2 anthology
Dark Confessions anthology
Freedom-Rapture anthology
Under Photon Crowns, chapbook by Dai Fry

2022

Nights on the Line – individual collection by M.S. Evans
Sun-Tipped Pillars Of Our Hearts anthology
Christmas & Winter Vol 3 anthology
Afterfeather anthology, edited by Briony Collins
Duet of Ghosts anthology, edited by Jen Feroze

2023

Sound and Vision, edited by Kitty Donnelly (online only)
Street Sailing – individual collection by Matt Gilbert
Tutankhamun Centenary anthology
The Poet Spells Her Name, by Sarah Connor
Christmas-winter edition Vol 4 anthology

2024

In flight anthology, edited by Marcelle Newbold

Publications by Matthew M. C. Smith

Origin: 21 Poems, by Matthew M C Smith (2018)
The Keeper of Aeons – Matthew M C Smith (The Broken Spine, 2022)
Pamphlet –- Paviland: Ice and Fire (Black Bough Poetry, 2023)

Forthcoming Titles

The Wasteland Centenary anthology (Black Bough 2024)
In the Shadow of Gods, collection by Rachel Deering (2024)
Collections by James McConachie and Louise Machen (2024)

About the cover artist

Emma Connolly is a multi, award-winning artist from Co. Wicklow, Ireland. She is a Master of Fine Art and has over 20 years experience as a professional artist. During this time, she has successfully exhibited internationally in New York, Cuba, Dublin & Berlin.

'As an artist, my work is a reflection of my deep connection to the natural world and my ongoing exploration of the interplay between light, texture, and colour. Drawing on over two decades of experience as a professional artist and a Master of Fine Art, I strive to create pieces that are both visually striking and emotionally resonant. My art is a celebration of the beauty and complexity of the world around us, and I am constantly inspired by the textures and patterns that I find in the natural landscape. Whether I am working with oils or mixed media, my goal is always to capture the essence of a particular moment in time, to create a window into the unique beauty of a place or a particular experience'

Website: www.emmaconnolly.me/, Instagram: www.instagram.com/connollyartist , X / Twitter: https://twitter.com/artemmaconnolly Facebook: www.facebook.com/emmaconnollyartist/

Permanent public collections on display, by Emma Connelly

Arts Council of Northern Ireland, MacNeice House, Belfast, N. Ireland
University Of Ulster, Belfast, N. Ireland
Jury's Hotel, Dublin, Ireland
Office of Public Works, Dublin, Ireland
Institute of Art, Design & Technology, Dun Laoghaire, Co. Dublin, Ireland.

About the authors / contributing editors

Gillian Clarke, poet, playwright, editor and translator was born in Cardiff, and now lives in Ceredigion. She was the National Poet of Wales 2008-16. Her poetry forms part of the English school syllabus in Britain and she was awarded the Queen's Gold Medal for Poetry in 2010 and the Wilfred Owen Award in 2012.

Yvonne Marjot is a lost Kiwi living on the Isle of Mull. Poet, author, librarian, escaped botanist, and now water-treatment operative: her poems are intimate and personal, and often link the natural world with mythological themes.

Merril D. Smith is a poet from southern New Jersey. Her collection, *River Ghosts*, was a *Black Bough Book* of the Month in Dec. 2022.

Rebecca Hooper is a writer and scientist. Her work is inspired by the threads that connect humans and other living things. She lives on a small Scottish island and can usually be found wandering the coast or in the sea.

Mark Antony Owen is the author of digital-only poetry project *Subruria*. His economic poems cycle through themes of love and loss and what we think we remember – shifting, unchronologically, between things observed and things recalled. Mark is also the creator, curator and driving force behind quarterly journal and poet library *iamb*, and ekphrastic poetry space *After* ...

David Hay's debut publication was the narrative poem 'Doctor Lazarus'. His debut poetry collection is forthcoming from *Rare Swan Press*. He has a collaborative work *Amor Novus/A Spontaneous Prayer* with *Soyos Books*, and pamphlet from *Back Room Poetry* out now and has a novel *How High the Moon* coming out from *Anxiety Press* later this year.

Robert Frede Kenter is a widely published writer, editor, visual artist, Pushcart Prize nominee and publisher of *Ice Floe Press*. A visual poetry collection, EDEN (2021, *Floodlight Editions*) is now available with *Rare Swan Press*.

Anne Phillips returned home after living on Ynys Môn for thirty years. She writes in both languages and has an MA in Creative Writing in Context from University of Bangor. Anne is working on her first collection.

Anna Chorlton writes in the Cornish wilds. She has poems in *Atlanta Review*, *Wild Court*, *Indigo Dreams*, *Ice Floe Press*, *Ink Sweat and Tears*, *Skylight 47*, *Black Bough* and *King River Press*. She is author of *Cornish Folk Tales of Place*.

Gayle J. Greenlea is an American-Australian writer, muso & counsellor for survivors of sexual & gender violence. Words in *Fevers of the Mind*, *Ice Floe Press* and *SAR*. Stands with a pen. @gjgreenlea@blsky.social @GJGreenlea@mstdn.social

Emma Jones is a writer, poet and mum of two toddlers based in Shropshire. She is passionate about the environment. Her work often focuses on nature and grief.

Karen Pierce Gonzalez's collections include *Coyote in the Basket of My Ribs* (*Kelsay Books*: 2023), *Down River with Li Po* (*Black Cat Poetry Press*: 2024), and *Sightings from a Star Wheel* (Origami Poems Project: 2024). KarenPierceGonzalez.blogspot.com

Iris Anne Lewis is widely published. Featured in *Black Bough's* Silver Branch Series, she enjoys running her poetry group, Wordbrew.

Matthew M. C. Smith's last collection was *The Keeper of Aeons*. He is campaigning for the return of the 'Red Lady' of Paviland (the remains of a 33,000 yr old Ice Age Hunter found in a Gower cave) from Oxford to Swansea. Twitter: @MatthewMCSmith Also on Insta and FB.

Glenn Barker writes about the complexity and raw edges of our human existence through imagism and impressionism; all in a futile attempt to understand his own psyche. He is a contributing reviewer to *Black Bough*. He also runs and sings. Twitter: @Glenn_A_Barker

Helen Openshaw is a Drama teacher from Cumbria. Words are in a variety of publications. Her first chapbook, 'A Revolution in the Sky' is published by *Alien Buddha Press*. Next year Helen will have a pamphlet published with *Hedgehog Poetry*. Twitter: @pocket_rhyme

Miles Hovey recently graduated from Aberystwyth University with a BA in Creative Writing. Previously he was a builder. He has been published by Literature Wales, *Collide Zine, Philadelphia, Black Bough Poetry* and the MA students' anthology, *Aberystwyth*. He is working on his first poetry collection.

Ness Owen lives on Ynys Mon. Her second collection *Moon Jellyfish Can Barely Swim* was published by *Parthian Books* in 2023. She was the winner of Greenpeace's *Poem for the Planet* 2022 and she co-edited the bilingual anthology *A470*.

Lesley Curwen has a pamphlet published with *Nine Pens*. She is published with *iamb, Ice Floe Press* and *After....*

Jared Mulhair is a husband, father, and spoken-word poet. He has performed his work across the Pacific Northwest US and has been published in *Consilience* and various international anthologies. You can snack on his manifold tweet-sized poems. Twitter: @PoeticAdept.

Regine Ebner is a teacher and writer in the American Southwest. Her work has been published by *Black Bough Poems*, *Loft Books*, *Cerasus Magazine*, *Spellbinder* and others. The beauty of the Sonoran Desert is often her muse.

Marcelle Newbold explores place and inheritance. Bridport Prize shortlisted, published by *IS&T*, *iamb*, *Fly on the Wall Press* and others. Cardiff, Wales. Twitter/ Insta: @marcellenewbold

Sarah Connor is a Pushcart/Best of Net nominee. Author of *The Crow Gods* and *The Poet Spells Her Name*. Twitter: @sacosw fmmewritespoems.wordpress.com Host of https://dversepoets.com/

Jo Dixon's poetry appears in a range of journals, including *The North* and *Modern Poetry in Translation*. *Purl (Shoestring)* was published in July 2020. Currently, she is exploring approaches to translation. Jo is a lecturer in creative writing at De Monfort University.

Saraswati Nagpal is an Indian poet, a writer of fantasy and sci-fi, and a classical dancer. Her graphic novels are feminist retellings of Indian myths. Her work is published or forthcoming in *The Atlantic*, *Atlanta Review*, *Acropolis Journal* and others. Social media: @saraswatinagpal

Printed in Great Britain
by Amazon

39802875R00020